Monologues and Lyrics

Poems by

Robert Wexelblatt

ISBN: 978-93-6354-844-2

First Edition: 2025
Rs. 200/-

Cyberwit.net
HIG 45 Kaushambi Kunj, Kalindipuram
Allahabad - 211011 (U.P.) India
http://www.cyberwit.net
Tel: +(91) 9415091004
E-mail: info@cyberwit.net

Printed at Repro India Limited.

Acknowledgments

"Mrs. Podolski at Four Score," "Mrs. Podolski on Brownings and Boys," "Mrs. Podolski on Democracy," "Mrs. Podolski on the Male Gaze," "Mrs. Podolski Picks over a Cliché and Søren Kierkegaard," "Mrs. Podolski Riffs on Reproduction," "Mrs. Podolski's Financial Advice," "Advice," "Anxiety Factory," "Brazilian Guitar Music," "Compare Down, Not Up," "If I've Told You Once," "Mrs. Oleander's Lovers," "Mrs. Oleander Goes Shopping," "Music Appreciation at Midnight," "A Professor in His Garden," "Suburban Silence,"
"Tomorrow's Poem" and "War Games of 1955" first appeared in *Verse-Virtual*

"A Beethoven Poem" and "Delusio Bene Esse" first appeared in *Gyroscope Review*

"At the Club" and "Fear in the Heroic Age" first appeared in *San Jose Studies*

"I Don't Want to Write Poetry" first appeared in *Midwest Poetry Review*

"Liebestod" first appeared in *Life As An [Insert Label Here]*

"Memento Mori" first appeared in *Young Ravens Literary Review*

"Musing at the Outdoor Early Music Festival" and "One Consolation" first appeared in *BlazeVOX*

"Nostalgia for November" first appeared in *Cimarron Review*

"Ointment" first appeared in *Carcinogenic Poetry*

"Six Snapshots of Social Life," "The Mogwai," and "Yuan-yang" first appeared in *Modern Literature*

"Hsi-wei Records Ten-Year-Old Mailing's Good Idea," "The War in the South," "The Silence of Hermits," and "Hsi-wei's Last Poem" first appeared in *Eastlit*

"Autumn in the Yellow Mountains" and "The Little Straw Sandals" first appeared in *Lowestoft Chronicle*

"On the Road Near Chiangling the Poet Chen Hsi-wei Encounters a Young Musician, Summer 597 A.D." first appeared in *Autumn Sky Poetry Daily*

"Yellow Moon at Lake Weishan" first appeared in *Mouse Tales*

"Hsi-wei in the Gardens of Shun" first appeared in *Offcourse Literary Journal*

"Hsi-wei's Justice" first appeared in *Otis Nebula*

Cover Credits: *Portrait of Elderly Woman,* Freepiks, 2025
Portrait of a Poet in a Landscape, Sitao, 1684, Wikimedia Commons

Contents

Mrs. Podolski at Four Score

Thank you, my dear, for the irises and
for remembering. If we weren't all in
thrall to decimal system I'd have
forgotten myself, and maybe just as well.

Threescore and ten's a term with biblical
authority. We forget the psalmist
didn't end there. In case anyone should
take pride in a reprieve, there's this codicil:
if…they be fourscore years, yet is their strength
labor and sorrow; for it is soon cut
off, and we fly away. I can't think of
anyone my age I'd call strong. Sorrow,
sure. But labor? They're all retired now,
grousing about the gumment, the grandkids,
or into a fresh childhood of their own.
Do you think I'm becoming childish too?
Well maybe, just without the innocence.

All week I've been thinking about my
parents, that I've lived longer than either
of them but how they'll always be older.
Even in an afterlife where precedence
doesn't count, I couldn't sit with them as
an equal. Even if we lounged around
playing bridge and watching Fifties re-runs,
I can't see myself claiming deeper wisdom.
Maybe this hard-and-fast seniority
is what's behind ancestor worship.

The father I adored and teased and
rebelled against, the mother I relied
on and neglected, this couple who
set me life's first problems and whom I loved
irregularly, are forever fixed
just like the snapshots in that album you
pored over last week. With Mr. P., it's
different. We were used to arguing,
agreeing, sharing. We slept hip to hip,
compeers, familiar with each other's smells
and tics, equals to the degree men and
women can be, together though not alike.
Podolski was laconic, a tightwad
with words, while I'm garrulous to a fault.

Your parents are still alive, dear, so changing,
as are you. Once you depended on them;
someday you may be their prop. You'll make a
stout one. I lean on you, you know, on your
willingness to listen to maundering
monologues like this, my self-indulgences.
How old women talk! If I thanked you as
much as you deserve, I'd bore you even more.

Apropos that album that so amused
you, it tickled me that it tickled you.
Someday soon I'll be frozen in a square
like that graduation photo for which
I refused to smile or the wedding
portrait with the forced grin and baroque hair.
You must have noticed the way photographs
displace the memories we tell ourselves
they preserve. We recollect what's fixed and final.

Death is as irremediable as that,
so we read backwards from the last chapter.

Worse than my mother's massive stroke in the
Winn-Dixie parking lot is what I've never
told you about my father. He was with me
last night, you know. Yes, the dead can come alive,
pay visits—not in seances but in
dreams. I don't think they're waiting beyond some
realm of fire but curled up in my limbic system.

I'm twice the age of my father when he
took out his Colt and weighed it in his hand.
Last night I dreamed the two of us were in
Delehanty's Bar on Stenton Avenue.
The place burned down decades ago. I can't
recall ever going inside so it was how
I imagined it—dimly lit, a sanctuary
for weary men and couples on the town.
It was a slow night. Workmen in muddy
pants and heavy boots slouched on the stools,
griping about the Dodgers moving west.
The barman cleaned glasses and let them
talk, nodding when they ordered one more round.
By the front window, a thirtyish couple
sipped whiskey sours and sniped at each other.
Father and I sat at the back, next to an
unplugged Seeburg where it was shadowy
and quiet. An eighty-year-old woman
across the table from a forty-year-old
man—anyone would take us for mother and
son. I told him as gently as I could
that the note he left wasn't good enough.

He seemed peeved. He'd typed it out. *To Whom It*
May Concern it started, followed by a
list of assets and liabilities,
then a perfunctory farewell. Even
his name was typed. I said I wanted a
better explanation. Was it money?
Angst? An insufferable diagnosis?
Despair? Unhappiness with Mother or with
me? Were we the cause or didn't we count
at all? Was it just one desperate drunken
impulse? He shook his head the way a coach
does when the batter's let him down. Even
at my age, three decades after the Change,
two after losing Podolski, that hurt.
It was useless pretending that, being
now his senior, a widow and old crone,
I could understand or help. I'm still his child.

My dear, nobody really knows about
dreams, where they come from or why. I wanted
to console him, lend comfort, solace,
to say something motherly and wise.
But what I absurdly wished to do, what
I really yearned to do, was change his mind.

Mrs. Podolski Makes A Distinction

What's the difference between solitude and
loneliness? Oh, my dear, I've had twenty
years to figure that one out.
                                        Solitude's
an old cotton sweater, large, comfy, that
wraps around you like a strong laconic
stud; loneliness is when it turns into
a hair shirt, a brute with a hangover
and the crabs. The difference, of course, is in
your skin and nerves, not the garment which is
merely a fact, a negative condition
that's often positive, that switches like
an electron leaping valences, some
shifty grimace/grin. Solitude's what you
yearn for when there's been a surplus of malls
and nieces, blab and book clubs, when the jam
and jar of houseguests have left you unnerved
and a quiet cup of tea appeals more
than a magnum and *côte de veau* at Le
Cirque, orchestra seats, a dinner with smart,
solicitous couples. Solitude you
rush home to but often it's loneliness
that lurks in the dark behind the sofa.
Solitude's a nice bath at two p.m.,
Dostoyevsky at midnight, in short a
luxury; or it's throwing yourself in
the nick of time onto the flagstones of
Notre Dame importuning for "*Sanctuaire*!"
Loneliness, though, is penitential

pinching in of walls, a cloister for the
faithless, the inescapable truth of
an emptiness that's utterly empty.

Socrates, my dear, is supposed to have
proved that tragedy and comedy are
one; but as no one was listening, sober
or awake, I guess he did it all alone.

Mrs. Podolski on Brownings and Boys

Another shooting at another school
this afternoon, another man-child with
an unbanned assault rifle, legal pistol,
his father's shotgun taking mad revenge
on the place that taught and demeaned him,
now desperate to massacre then die, a
kamikaze menace to innocents
and protectors, police and principals.
Never a woman, notice. These gargoyles,
fresh-faced or hairy, remind me of that
indigestible bit of dialogue
from the German playwright Johst. *Whenever*
I hear the word culture I release the
safety on my Browning. It's from a play
he wrote for Hitler's forty-fourth birthday
in 1933 and the only
line he's sort of known for. Sort of? That's
because it's usually both misquoted and
misattributed. No wonder people
think it was said by Goering or Himmler.
Hanss Johst was the Nazis' laureate.
He must have reached for his gun often as
the bastard wasn't short on culture.
He studied medicine, philosophy,
even art history. I'm sure he studied
hard too, like the thorough Teuton he was.
Johst ended up expiring in an old folk's
home in 1978. How do
I know all this, my dear? Well, the Nazi

bard would be tickled to know he rates his
very own Wikipedia page.

My dear, education's no guarantee
of decency. Germany was chockfull
of *herr doktors*. It's so often schools
get shot up, and usually the ones that taught
the shooters. Isn't it curious that
Hanss Johst specified an all-American
Browning and not what Fannie Schultz would call
eine wirklich deutsche Luger? It's as though he
sensed America was the true home of
the killer's kit. The Browning Company
was founded in 1878 in
Ogden, Utah, by a clot of brothers.
John did the inventing. Ogden has
a museum dedicated to the
company, all sorts of lethal toys for
cowboys, Mormons, Marines, deranged dropouts.
It has a Dinosaur Park, too.
What do
you think, my dear? Do these hateful gunmen
aim at children because it was children
who shunned them? Because it's more newsworthy
than blowing away middle-aged shoppers?
I picture a festering tumor
of resentment and humiliation
rising brainwards for years, juiced by social
media. I see them crouched over laptops
in rank bedrooms, their parents' damp cellars,
plotting their moves, fondling the legal guns,
dreaming of the satisfaction they'll feel,
going out in glory, winning sympathy
they'll never get, not the anathema

they'll earn. They pump out manifestoes like
French artists, megalomaniac
justifications, self-pitying,
bile-soaked, letters to the world.
Like Johst, they cleave to the crude organizing
principle of hate. As I remember
it, girls stuff such griefs inside, push them down, grab
the rocky road, not the revolver.

In German, *pistole* is female, yet
it's always the boys who reach lovingly
for one. There are those who never get over
the mortification of sixth grade,
the misery of adolescence, the
boys who shoved, the girls who whispered and
giggled behind their hands.
The parents claim
to be stunned. They might have fretted, may have
shrugged off the evidence, hoping there
would be a job, a girl, a wedding.

Never again, mouth the grownups again,
but it sounds like a forlorn prayer, part of
a ritual, not an oath, an act,
nothing to threaten Browning's profits.
A civilized country would ban the things,
also diesel engines and leaf blowers.
Meanwhile, waiting in closets and kitchen
drawers are millions of Brownings, thousands of
twisted minds, hundreds of hands keen to
release the safety. And it's always
the boys, never the girls. What was that, my dear?
Oh yes. So far.

Mrs. Podolski on Democracy

My dear, it's all right. Go ahead, talk politics.
I guess you got a shock when Brenda told you
how she's going to vote and then—let me know
if I'm wrong—started to proselytize.
No, no need to apologize. Politics
is mostly talk, but that's not to say the
talk's inconsequential. In fact, I think
people don't do it enough—I mean to
each other, I mean informed conversations,
without the slogan-cudgels and
sawed-off bumper stickers.
So, you
mentioned democracy and Brenda scoffed?
Well, democracy may not be as fragile as
Brenda is cynical. You know those tires
that seal themselves around six-inch nails?
Democracy's self-correcting too; you
can make a change without killing anybody.
The Athenians kept it going for
a while. You could vote on everything so
long as you weren't female or a slave.
What, my dear? Females and slaves. Isn't it what
you meant by the word with all those syllables?
What was it? Oh yes, intersectionality.
Anyway, Athens' sort of voting's risky,
short-term thinking, passing passions. Since
Socrates, no philosopher's had a
good word for direct democracy,
not even Rousseau. Plato hated it

all, and dreamed of a city ruled by
unelected geometers. One size
fits all. Aristotle, born middle-aged
and a biologist, knew better. Knew what?
That no good society is perfect, dear,
and no perfect society is good.
You like my uninspiring one-liner?
Good. Up next? The pre-imperial Romans.
Once they'd packed Tarquin off, they ruled themselves
decently for centuries with a constitution
durable as one of their arches.
One senate, two parties, and a brace of
consuls, even tribunes for the legions,
traders, and the unwashed hoi polloi.
Aristocratic and authoritarian? Sure,
and patriarchal too—but there was
no tyranny. It worked until they started
conquering like addicts, amassing their empire,
which led to Julius then a whole centuries
of Caesars.

People are sure they're free and that
their forebears weren't. To historians
history always looks inevitable.
Demosthenes could have told them that empires
cry out for emperors. Can you picture
our City Council trying to run half
of Europe? Still, it's touching how Romans
kept up the republican fiction for years,
as if to admit the truth would shame them,
as if their stern ancestors would rise up
pointing.

So, democracy, you said.
I can hear Brenda's dismissive little

pfft. It's thanks to her our democracy
really does feel fragile. Franklin warned us
on Day One. There are always Brendas
to tell us we're not perfect, or even good.
Those traditions and institutions we liked
to think were stable as a pyramid
are wobbling, attacked, violated, called
shams or worse. Courts, public education,
regular elections, and a free press.
I'm worried
and you are too, my dear, or Brenda
wouldn't have gotten to you, made you
anxious that liberty and the rule of law
are desiccated, like hollow reeds waiting
to be cut down.
Ironic it should be
conservatives behind it, the new kind
I mean, who don't aim to conserve anything.
A few years back, one of the old sort prophesied
that, if his zealous colleagues couldn't win
democratically, it's democracy
they'd give up on, not their aims. No, they'd hug
those all the tighter to their heaving chests,
their withered dugs. Sound at all like Brenda?
I'm thinking of my own pal, Mrs. Debeque.
Sweet woman. Last week we also got to
talking politics. Ruth likes the Constitution
and all the amendments but said her favorite's
the nineteenth and that she loves voting, the
lining up, the democratic queue
of plumbers, secretaries, waitresses,
seamstresses, porters. She doesn't hold with
voting by mail. She says it isn't

democratic enough because you don't
get to smell your fellow citizens. I
asked how she chooses a candidate.
"Oh, that's easy," said Ruth. "I just ask Charlie
who he's for then vote for somebody else."

Mrs. Podolski on the Male Gaze

I take your point, my dear. How could I help
but feel indignant for your sake, mad at
that jerk for—what was your word? Right,
objectifying you. You're not a floor
lamp or a Maserati.
                                        We're all
subjects to ourselves of course, and men would
do well to acknowledge that. Agreed.
But haven't we looked in mirrors all our
lives? Appraised ourselves before stepping out?
Aren't we then objects to ourselves?
                                                            Men can't
help checking out women—or women men,
if they're honest. It's natural or, as you'd say,
programmed in. But it's *how* men look and how
we *read* their staring. Wrong looks make us think
of what they'd like to do to us—*to*, not *with*.
But, take it from me, the day you stop being
an object isn't a red-letter one.
In the Middle Ages, holy days were marked
on calendars with red letters. You'll find
when that day comes, my dear, years and years from
now, the first letter won't be red.
                                                        Most men
do fall short, though. I'm thinking of all
those male painters aiming at beauty but
turning out pretentious pornography.
You've seen their odalisques. Give me an old
woman by Rembrandt any day. That man

could paint from the inside out. He'd pour as much
effort into the portrait of a crone
like me as one of his much-loved Saskia.
What's blamable, offensive, obnoxious, isn't
the male gaze but when it's no more than that.

When I was your age, presentable and
unmarried, two men at work took an interest—
but in such different ways. Both were single
and I had yet to meet Podolski.
Herb praised my outfits and my hair, but he
was leering elsewhere, so his compliments
felt like insults. But Roger, well Roger
looked too, but he didn't leer. He never
complimented anything about me.
On the contrary, he found fault with what
virtues I had as much as with my flaws.
He belittled my work, mocked my accent,
scoffed at my opinions. And yet somehow,
my dear, somehow all his insults felt like
compliments.

What? Me and Roger? Oh yes.

Mrs. Podolski Picks Over A Cliché and Søren Kierkegaard

My decrepit friends dipped their balding heads
and sighed at that line about how, at
the end, it's all those things you didn't do
you regret, and never the ones you did.
It's not just crones with expired sell-by
dates who kowtow to this deep wisdom; even
the young and smooth, like you, do too. You've heard
it, my dear? Yes, I thought as much. Well, who
dares contest the authority of the
moribund? Superstition bars dissent.
To demur wouldn't be just bad luck but bad
taste, speaking ill of the practically dead.
So, people buy it, bow, file it under
received wisdom. After all, it's plausible.
Surely all illusions evaporate
in the final hours. Why not caution and
scruples too? It's unsettling but easy
to imagine yourself ruing the things you
didn't do when you're about to lose the
chance to do anything at all. Like what?
Celia said not sleeping with the tennis
pro, and passing up an Alaskan cruise.
Hannah and Giulia made a catalogue:
not buying the Dior, not learning German,
Italian, Hebrew, mahjong, not bolting
from the altar or at least telling
Horace's mother to shut up for once.
To the licentious, *do it now or else*

will sound like license. But it's all absurd.
There were reasons for not shacking up
with the young stud, not embezzling from
the mean employer, not running the
Boston marathon, not absconding with
some hirsute pothead in a VW van.
If, before the gate of unbeing, people
had done all those things they thought they might
regret not doing, I'm sure they'd bemoan
what they did far more than what they didn't.
It's bookish teenagers say your choices
define you. *Philosophy 103:*
Existentialism for the Immature,
flattering egos still short of prefrontal
cortex. Well, my dear, I say we make our
choices, not vice versa as though somebody
else were yanking the strings. But, to be fair,
it's a distinction without a lot of
difference as the outcome's the same
either way. The first existentialist said
you can make sense of your life in reverse
but have to live it in drive. He managed
to motor in both gears, chewing over
his own choices for years so that rumination
became his life. He jettisoned the girl
he loved then indited page after
profound page about it, which he could
do having chosen writing over wedlock.
You might say the man didn't marry in
order to write books about not getting
married. And yet he denied the choice was
his, even though it made him what he was.
No, he laid the responsibility

on God who vetoed the nuptials,
assigning him a monastic mission for
which he was ideally fitted and
which, by his own reckoning, he fulfilled.
He only lived to forty-two, you know,
about half my age. No, I don't believe
he regretted much as he lay a month dying
in Copenhagen's Frederik's Hospital.
If he had regrets, he'd recorded them
already and at length. Oh yes, and what
of the jilted fiancée? She wasted no
time before getting hitched to someone
else, her former tutor yet, an old story.
If there were last-minute compunctions, I
think it was she who had them, regrets
for what he didn't choose, for what she did,
or both. Sad. Isn't it sad? An ending
without happiness, a rom com in reverse.

My dear, I'm sorry for blathering on
like some superannuated pedant
who ought to have retired when everyone
else thought she should. She'd have plenty of time
for regrets then, wouldn't she? She could feel
bored, useless, and sorry that she quit. Or,
professing to the very end, she could
regret that too, what with yawning students
and crudely plagiarized essays to grade.

Well, *basta*! What I'm regretting now is
this maundering to which you're too sweet to
put a stop. What I might regret later,
even without a deathbed under me,

isn't just boring you but doing it
without offering tea and cake. So, how
about I put the kettle on and cut
us each a big slice of angel-food. . . .
As if angels eat!

Mrs. Podolski Riffs on Reproduction

Ruth Debecq was complaining about old ladies
being invisible. Well, of course, I said.
It's not disdain; it runs gene-deep.
Those ripe to procreate draw the eyes
even of old women, certainly of men.
Life wants more of itself, doesn't care
about Ruth's vanity, let alone
her dignity. Life wants more of itself and,
if possible, better. Mistakes will be
discarded later. That's what drama's
about, you know, families, sex and death.
One gets us here, the other gets us out.
The tragedy's that Hamlet and Ophelia
never make Hamlet the Third. That family's
wiped out, Act Five, Scene Eleven, pfft!
The comedy's knowing Elizabeth
and Darcy will furnish Pemberly with an
heir—though I'd prefer an heiress. You too?
It's the fertile, the nubile draw the eye,
the gossip, paparazzi, pubescent boys,
crones who lunch, incontinent codgers.
It's not just lust, life's tool. On them depends
the species' survival, maybe an upgrade.
Biologically speaking, females are
visible when they can bear children,
less so once they do, when there's less autonomy,
more hemming in. To the young, the future
should look promising. But those awake
to global warming and the national debt

resent their elders, even the ones who
cherish them, who've fed, clothed, educated,
and spoiled them. Many rebel, it seems,
make a choice in favor of more choices
by a sort of self-sterilization.
Adolescence is a battle between
culture and hormones. Hormones don't always
win out, it seems. Middle age has many
markers, my dear. My favorite is the
moment you hear yourself complaining
more about the next generation than
the last one. Watch yourself for that, dear.

Nowadays, the more advanced a country,
the lower its birthrate. My clever friend
Leah Shapiro used to teach English
poetry. Now that she's retired, she makes
more of it. Last week, she gave me some verses,
just doggerel but it got me thinking.
She said she was piqued by a BBC
article and took the headline for her title.
"Sexless in Japan" she calls it.
I've got it here. Shall I read it to you? Yes?

Young Nipponese
with exposed knees
the J-Pop flirts
wear real short skirts
or leather pants
and tops from France.
High on ganja
steeped in manga
they've got tiny noses
eyes like black roses

work way too late
for a midnight date.
Mother or father?
way too much bother.
So, Japan's gone id-less
and nearly kid-less—
not to mention Yid-less.
That last line's Leah all over.
She says she feels Jewish around gentiles
and gentile when she's with Jews. The woman
has five grandchildren. Well, I have no children—
if we except you, my dear. Of course,
you're somebody else's daughter, but mine
by election. Well no, I'm more of a
grandmother, aren't I? Leah says grandparents
get all the upside and none of the down,
love without responsibility.
Grandmothers are the old wives whose tales are
full of disinformation. Grandmothers
might make good midwives, I guess. But really,
who cares about grandmothers? If they're not
unseen and silent, they chatter away
interminably—just like me, like now,
and always to you, dear. Invisible,
of little use. But you, my dear, you
must be the most patient of twenty-somethings.
Everyone sees you. Throat, legs, chest, hips, hair.
Everybody. Here's looking at you, kid.

Mrs. Podolski's Financial Advice

Did I call money the first consideration?
Well, not if the drapes are on fire, of course.
But, in general, yes. Though it's upstairs that
we work, eat, and sleep, houses need foundations.
Still, the first consideration isn't always
the most important, dear, as when you need
the Honda keys to get to your wedding.

Lucre's not filthy, just what the Bishop
of Hippo called an occasion of sin.
If I remember Father Staszic's lesson right,
pecunia non est radix omnium
malorum, sed avaritia. The sin's not
in the woman but her lust-drunk ravisher.

Mrs. Riley likes to serve up the obvious
as wisdom, warming up somebody else's
casserole as if it were her own and made
from scratch. The other day, after the usual
ten minutes of retailing her ill-health, she
declared with high sagaciousness that it's
easy to be young and strapped, but not to be
both old and poor. *Duh*, as your friend Brenda
would say. I loved that, by the way. *Duh.*
The curt dismissiveness of the syllable,
tongue up against the teeth, a fine derisive
plosive, the posing at stupidity.
Well, I suppose saying *Duh* was original
once, then—in a week—one more cliché.

Anyway, Mrs. Riley was only half right.
The Rileys were always flush; young or old,
she's never run low, never felt that shame.
Money's merely means, my dear. Making it
an end turns life into an accounting game.

Well, since you've asked, let's have a drink,
And then I'll tell you what I think.
A sherry or your usual Earl Grey tea?
Please pour a finger of Laphroaig for me.
It won't take long to state my views—
then, we can scoff at the evening news.

Earn what you need to pay your bills
and mind you never pay them late.
Don't take risks for a higher rate
or lust after wealth's mirages—
Rodeo Drive, Beverly Hills,
McMansions with four-car garages.

The rich with too much in the bank
are twins to those without a dime;
both are imprisoned by their rank
and think of money all the time.
So, not too much and not too little;
I find life's better in the middle.

Best of all is having the wherewithal
not to think about the wherewithal
at all.

A Beethoven Poem

In a Bad Mood

His head's been aching in B-minor.
Carters are quarrelling down on Mölker Bastel.
Sultry air, rotting pears, stupid barons,
French officers strutting down the Graben.
Frustration courses through his left hand;
the fingers of the right scamper but
never more than an octave above middle C.
He batters his new Broadwood
forte not *piano*, more drum than harp.
He's already demolished four instruments.
Half-a-dozen false endings build
power equal to a Napoleonic assault.
Against the brick wall of the world
he hurls syncopations, fractured motifs,
cracks conventions and, with a grimace,
whips his wrath to indignant beauty.
Robbed of his liberal hopes and perfect pitch,
his liver's bad, digestion worse,
the soup too salty, and the penny lost.

In a Profound Mood

He knows it's coming nearer, feels it
during long Vienna nights. He writes
as if to greet it a music of the future.
The caesuras between notes are
poignant; chords deepen as they linger.
The inward soliloquies in the late sonatas,
confabulations of the last quartets, lug
us to feelings we didn't know could be had,
conduct us through the doorway of
a house far grander than Pasqualati's,
through the gate of a city too high to be
seen even from the Hofburg's domes.
What his soul hears, we'll hear only with our ears.
Music fashioned from silence, lost love, spent sound,
drape a soft blanket over anguish, resignation.
Piercing deeper, ever more sublime, rarefied,
his harmonies of restrained might make
mortality itself nearly tolerable. Nearly.

In a Good Mood

A C-major day, neither flat nor sharp,
fine weather for November. The jolly rondo
slipped out smoothly, faster than he could
write it down, an easy birth; variations
tumbled over one another like the
Hoffmanns' new kittens. At dinner, there
had been bread soup, his favorite,
prepared by the faithful Sali who
possesses the requisite purity of heart.
Later, he'd be joining Seyfert for
two or three glasses of Spätburgunder.
Good old Ignaz! He laughs out loud recalling
the prank he'd played on the fellow,
asking him to turn the pages at the premiere
of the new concerto when they all were blank.
What a cadenza he invented that night!
Afterwards, at zum Weissen Schwann,
everybody had howled at the joke.
Ignaz, making an unforgettable face,
grudgingly allowing that it was droll.
Now, for a change, his stomach is at peace.
Wanting a lungful of cold, fresh air,
he walks to the window, throws back the
shutters, and leans far out into the dusk.
A dozen boys are sprinting jubilantly down
the Schreyvogelgasse, galloping home to
tasty dinners, grumpy fathers, forgiving mothers.

Advice

Let those in, but stay outside;
close the door, but not too wide.

Bestir yourself while you're at rest;
your worst is better than your best.

They've patched the road around the hole;
you're well-heeled now, save for your soul.

The car's all gassed, the sky's black blue;
the clock runs backwards, three to two.

One meal a day makes not a fast;
an unstruck match is made to last.

Leave rooms that cough, they seethe with germs;
fish you can catch are full of worms.

You'd have two legs if you could dance;
don't wear a skirt beneath your pants.

Endure the weather, bear the news;
regret the future, rent the pews.

Let them all in after you go;
if they say yes, then you say no.

Anxiety Factory

I've never known him fretless, unapprehensive, free of worry.
Plein de soin when he visited Paris, in Vienna *voller Fürsorge.*
Were he born Roman, equestrian or plebeian, he'd be
plena cura—Carthaginians, a failed harvest in Egypt, yet
more civil war, Huns, a restless wife shopping for henbane.
Occasions aren't scarce—his divorce, the kids, psychotic
girlfriend, neurotic second wife, fishy looks at work, his
IRA, the next vacation, nuclear and climate bombs, black
mold in the basement, needing to pee four times a night.

The busy little plant features lathes and forges, cogs and presses,
die cutters, extruders, nozzles, flanges, a furnace with a miniature
smokestack pumping angst's waste straight into the large intestine.
Though invisible even to an MRI, I picture the works nestled
a smidgin right of his stomach, just left of the gallbladder.

The factory never closes down, switches shifts, takes no breaks.
Overnight, it churns out nightmares, horrors and catastrophes
fabricated from memories, burritos, pad thai, shrimp scampi.
It won't rest on a Sabbath or high holiday, let alone a long
weekend. The thing is autochthonous, automated, self-lubricat-
ing, ununionized, and warranted to work unremittingly for life.

At the Club

The afternoon was ripe with women
dressed in white on green divans,
suave men beneath the awnings talking
of trade and pars. The bar's two fans
were stirring breezes blue as the sound of ice
striking glass across the turquoise patio
where shade trees bent. "How nice,"
you said, how nice it all is," then
you turned about, smiling on everything.
But mostly you were touched by the soft hands
of the man at the piano, the one whose wife
had, so unexpectedly, taken her own life.

Brazilian Guitar Music

Music is the mediator between the spiritual and sensual life. . . .The guitar is a miniature orchestra in itself.
-Ludwig van Beethoven

This music unwinds, reassures, consoles,
almost convinces me that I'm Brazilian,
speak softened Portuguese, relish beaches,
casual sex, and samba, don't need
to rush anxiously from there to here, can
meander gracefully, languid yet fit.

I revere Mozart but he never makes
me feel Salzburgian, Schubert like
a native Viennese, or Bach a pious
Lutheran. Poulenc, on the other hand,
will francomorph me, and Milhaud can turn
me French and Brazilian at once. Strange
how a few chords change me into a laid-back
Brazuca or acerbic boulevardier
who loiters nonchalantly in bistros.

I suppose my auditory complex
is standard issue, like anyone else's.
So, the magic must be in the limbic
system, an amygdala or hippocampus
that is all my own. Melodies summon
the lush life of Sao Paulo and Rio,
the clear-cut pastures of Para, the
rainforests of Mato Grosso. My soles

sense the white sands of Baio do Sancho,
though I've never been south of Delray Beach.

The invigorating miscellany
of skin colors, the countrywide mingling
of genes, is both shame and glory, one
become the other. All those deported
degradados spread out, raping their way
across a domain ninety-two times
bigger than home, exercising *o direito*
do senhor like Argave *latifundariários.*

Africa's here too, sounds of the ensnared
and enslaved who would not forget the beats
of a *djembe*, the plucked notes of a *Mbira*.

Músicas de guitarra cool in August,
are cozy in February, unclench the mind's
fist, transmute old bitterness to nostalgia.
Here's a sweetness hinting that even
brutality might someday modulate
into a noble promiscuity.

Compare Down Not Up

Not the big shot with the Harvard chair,
But the weary adjunct with the dirty hair.

Not the comely, cool, adored rock star,
But the nasty drunk tossed from the bar.

Not the plutocrat in a splurging mood,
But the guy with a sign: *Will Work for Food.*

Not the Dalai Lama and not the Pope,
But the orphan without a home or hope.

Delusio Esse Bene

As you step on to the pavement
after bearing the dentist's quest
for profitable trouble, a
scrutiny that, for once, turned up
neither cavities nor decay,
no plausible case for root
canal, just the head shake and the
ineluctable *We'll have to*
keep an eye that bicuspid,
teeth scraped clean to innocence
by the meticulous, only
mildly scolding hygienist
who scoured a smile so bright
you feel like you've dropped half a pound's
worth of plaque—you're confident of
your invulnerability,
sure that even a careening bus
would miss you, that a deranged drunk
on the subway wouldn't single
you out or have a knife, and that
when you get home there's bound to be
something more delightful than a
fistful of bills in the mailbox.

You've fixed the veneer that detached
from the kitchen cabinet with
contact cement and it looks
just fine, nobody's going to guess
that it was ever flapping free

and looking cheap, they won't even
know it's just veneer, while you'll be
congratulating yourself for
how smart it was thinking to use
contact cement, so you saunter
from room to room breathing deeply,
bowels at ease, alimentary
canal and lungs in good trim
that will be as everlasting
as that cabinet's bogus oak.

The myrtle you picked out at the
garden store as ground cover for
your blotchy backyard looks all right,
unwilted, the garden maven
swore it would spread, stay green all
winter, be verdant by next spring
when periwinkle blooms will burst
and you're certain you'll be alive
to see them erupt come April.

After half an hour of frenzied
searching the two couches, under
three chairs, four drawers, and two beds, you
finally find the lost remote
and all at once the feng shui
of familiarity is
restored, now everything is just
where it ought to be, nothing will
ever get misplaced again, just
as that can of Flex-Seal will keep
the cellar dry forever more.

The last grandson's graduated,
you survived all his finals, term
papers, even the senior thesis,
so you suppose you're immortal.

Two hours in and at last you've
hit on *le mot juste*, grinning
at that word, you're certain
the rest of the poem will slide
out smoothly like an easy birth.

Fear in the Heroic Age

We cherish it as if it were tomorrow.
The grapeshot rain, the boulder wind,
us barking up the isinglass rocks
lung to lung, how the night was ripped like
a black envelope, our white manifestos
scrawled across the deep violet sky.
That night our complexions cleared.
That week we thought, “We were made for this.”
That month our soft puerile bodies grew hard.
That season we learned to think and love and smoke.
In a lull, Tommy wrote his theodicy.
He’s a live stockbroker now,
but then he was a dead man who explained
the tuberose, Verdun, mosquitos,
Disneyland hell, Chief-Joseph heaven.
God, Tommy wrote, sits on the sidelines behind
ranks of cherubim with golden pompoms
forming nine-layered pyramids, leading cheers.

We battled on for weeks in mists,
in hail and sleet; we felt like Danae
and nobody admitted catching cold
or wanting food or hearing women cry.
We edited our slogans that made it
plain how the world’s cumulate injustice
had spun to this single point,
this instant when the anagnoritic bull at
last ignored the cheating cape and gored
the fake brocade with his critique.

Muscular, poor, awake at 4 a.m.,
boogying under fire, singing to distill
sweet implausible nostalgia. Oh yeah.

There was only one fear and it grew
on us like lichen, impossible to
brush off, dirty and tough; it crept over
us like cold daybreak, stupid and grey
as lead, making our eyes itch and our
guts tremble; it took us over like a
tomcat a vole, an idiot gun
a brilliant riposte, a nasty truth a
delicious lie. Now we have mementos,
old fringed armbands and frayed puttees, our
unhinged shades and U.S. Keds, a few
snapshots of militant fists, blurred grins,
faces that don't even resemble our kids'.
We knew it couldn't last.
We feared we'd outlast it.

I Don't Want To Write Poetry

For one thing, there's already too much of
it, not just of the bad but, worse yet, of
the good. Can't imagine what makes people
want to write the stuff, vanity I guess,
tweezing their feelings, laying them down on
black velvet to be foiled, boxed, admired.
Obscure poems are odious with their will
to be abstruse but obvious ones are
still worse. If there's one thing I don't want to
do it's write a poem. Anyway, I can't.
Swinging a bat hardly makes you the Babe.
My stomach's turned by poets who punctuate
drunkenly, the oddballs who scatter
lines crazily over the page, also
bombastic bards capitalizing like
mad Germans, hirsute rhapsodic types
inflated like barrage balloons. Even the
laconic are wasting somebody's time.
What nerve it takes to write, not merely a
single poem (anybody might be
forgiven one) but entire hecatombs,
whole passels of them, collecting and
selecting like a child messing in
its own filth: *Look, Mommy! See what I made!*
To write half of a poem is digging half
a hole, you sink further in the more you
work—work of a kind, though it's surely
easier to write a bad poem than to
dig a good hole. Moreover, no one asked

me for a poem and every schoolgirl can
tell you what happens when supply outstrips
demand. Who wants to wield a pointless spade?
Frankly, I'd sooner balance my checkbook,
take a nap, rake up a mound of leaves then
invite the local brats to jump in them.
They'd squeal with glee. At least that does the heart
good unlike listening to poets intone
their verses, another thing I can't see
doing, painfully enunciating
syllable after priceless syllable,
declaiming line by florid line, their
mouths twisting to self-satisfied smirks
after every metaphor then, at last,
in unctuous silence, moved and panting,
almost throwing up their arms like trapeze
artists who make you think they nearly fell.

If I've Told You Once

Don't stick your finger in there.
People won't like you if you brag.
Sit there until you finish your peas.

But the socket's so alluring and
it was my first time down the slide.
As for the squishy peas—they're not mine.

Civilization batters down the gates
with the voice of a mother, sets up
its occupying garrison, settles in

until the occupier becomes not
just another citizen but the mayor.
Yet sometimes a child recalls, rebels,

convenes a meeting, informs the voters
their mayor's an interloper whose
alien rules can justly be ignored.

But no, they say, he's one of us.
But no, they say, there would be guilt.
You're just a kid, they say. Grow up.

Liebestod

The still bedroom was dimmed by blue drapes.
Though they were outside time it mattered
it should be a November afternoon
when exertion brought its own reward.
He was an expiring salmon expending the
last erg of energy in the sweet water
of his birth; wave on wave buoyed him
then dropped until he plumbed the
matrix of all metaphor, perishing
with limbs of lead into the dusky void—
only to renew the compulsive cycle
of recurrence heralded by Nietzsche,
framed by Klimt, explicated by Freud.

Was it the love of death,
the death of love, or merely one
soul lost in the release of spirit,
the love that feels like death?

Memory shuffles delight up with regret.
When did the Lovedeath turn to the death of
love, the death of love to the love of death?
Was it in the middle of a sentence
or in the silence between breath and breath?

Memento Mori

To beseeching Lycaon Achilles said
that one morning, noon, or night he'd be dead,
even he, the most invincible of men,
though he couldn't say precisely how or when.

Prometheus must have believed in progress.
He gave us fire—medicine, metallurgy,
ships and shampoo—yet he left us to guess
the date of our deaths, bestowing blind hope,
his last gift, condition of using the rest,
the boon of ignorance that helps us cope.
Progress? Sure, though not for him, not for those
chained to the knowledge that they're food for crows.

There's a majesty in the dying year,
a poignant sepia-saturated
acceptance, a dignity beyond fear.

Ever wonder while watching the last brown
leaves leaving black branches, spiraling down,
or wake to frost and think of all that's past—
whether next November will be the last?

Mrs. Oleander's Lovers

At fifteen, lots of boys ogled her bust
and butt, eyes smeared with adolescent lust.
Empowered by their infatuation,
she cherished her sketchy reputation.

In college, she joined a sorority
where sex was the top priority.
The sisters tacked condoms to their door.
All did well, but she earned the highest score.

Mr. O. gave her an American
Express card, two weeks at a Sheraton,
her white Mercedes, Lagerfeld dresses,
a mansion, a pool—but few caresses.

She ran through men as she ran through money,
coupling like some concupiscent bunny.
Casual affairs gave her something to do;
After a month, she'd need somebody new.

There was just one she found hard to forget,
but the longing soon waned, then the regret.

Mrs. Oleander Goes Shopping

She looks, she buys,
grabs passing highs
from shelves, off racks,
new tops, fresh slacks,
lipstick, perfume,
sweet hat, posh phone.

Her closet's full of costly things.
She has a taste for scarves and rings.
A Meissen nymph, a Luxeire blouse
don't make a home, just gild the house.

Substituting footgear for needs
breeds an avid thirst that feeds
on itself, unslaked by stuff.
Blahnik and Prada aren't enough.

Music Appreciation at Midnight

Once again Yo-Yo Ma performs the
Suites for the first time, animates them just
for me. This is what a single bow
can do, two hands, four strings, two noble minds.

Ma plays; I take in as much as I can
grasp. He's deep inside the Hispanic dance
for German angels. This last sarabande's
inside him too. As for me, I press my
face up against a double-glazed window.

The faces of cellists, violinists
pianists as they play ecstatically,
their nodding to the rhythms of the
sublime, the strain of major muscles and
minuscule nerves—all this we look on with
gratitude and a measure of envy.
We want to have what they're having.

I am moved at three Platonic removes:
Bach, Ma, then, far, far off to the side...me.

Musing At The Outdoor Early Music Festival

To be the Bach-begetting race
long after we and earth are dead
we shot his preludes into space—
bragging, as Lewis Thomas said.

Music is math plus mystery,
organized improvisation,
its source beyond both history
and Euterpe's inspiration

in misery, collaboration,
a hundred mouths, a single brain
too dead to hear an ovation,
brightness of trumpets, plash of rain.

Whatever we feel we can sing and by
that singing cause others to feel; our art's
a looping feedback of joy and despair,
stateliness and laughter, ample harvests in
soothed pain, rowdy glee, agreeable shocks
of scintillation. Shamed by so many
of our acts, we're always proud of our stories,
our joyful noises, the ways we crank up
the mute rainbows of our lives by dreaming
plots and harmonies, at once ephemeral
and permanent like extinct creatures sealed
in the amber of dark vanished forests.

Nostalgia for November

E-minor was its key, that symphony
of abbreviated days and extruded
nights expelled like ascending divers' breaths,
pedal-point, kettle-drum and cello doling
darkness in sooty baritone. People
charged into the streets aiming their shoulders
like fullbacks racked by mid-season aches. All
work, no play, fraternal grimaces were
few, like those of sailors sweating at the
pump of some sinking sloop; yet under your
shapeless jumper must have been those holy
places I could tell off one by one but
had no warrant to see or smell or stroke.
Solitary pathos, there's a cliché
compels no pity. Whoever does not
long to be loved, pleads for no perpetual
proofs, he's held wise; yet such wisdom feels like
death's first teasing tickle. The boring film
of crowds flashing by in subway frames
reiterates that life is need, is need,
is the endless panting to have. Were there
a saint among them, one of the thirty-six
just men, even he would shiver in the
descending chill, would for a promise of
love disclose his secret identity,
the Atlas shudder each chilled accountant
and secretary dreads. In bared branches I
glimpsed your naked arms; in the music store
the adagio maestoso of your

curved back; in the braying of drunken
freshmen, the rapture of ancient autumns.
Beside such vigorous folly even
hard-bought wisdom yields poor consolation.

Ointment

The hedges are trimmed and the grass
mown; all is green and flat around
the birdbath's pedestal; myrtle

and violets flourish beneath
the magnolia and pines. The bathroom
tiles gleam; the desk is dust-free,

the kitchen counters spotless as the
bamboo floor, the Shiraz rug, your
lungs and conscience. You've exercised,

sweated, showered, and nobody's
phoned to raise alarms. Well-being
suffuses the summer afternoon

which is silent, blue. You're half through
Conrad's *Rover*; *Les Enfants du
Paradis* waits for nightfall on

a silver disk. You recall Brahms's
Second Serenade in your ears
as you biked beside a pasture,

three horses, how she used to smile.
Sparrows and butterflies rejoice.
Regret's been crammed into a drawer.

Your work's gone well; one hour after
dinner should suffice to finish.
Because nothing seems wrong, time stops.

One Consolation

As we grow older so the world grows
more complex, and more forgetful too,
as if wisdom and ignorance joined hands,
pressed cheeks, and staggered through a clumsy dance
to time's swift jigs and slow sarabandes.
Life's banal days and undistinguished nights
must not be despised since they're all we can
return to from our odysseys, our flights
through exotic latitudes, from our dreams.
Though quotidian tunes weary our ears
with routine rhythms punctuating years,
such music's always sweeter than it seems.

A Professor in His Garden

takes a solitary postprandial
stroll reviewing his vegetable troops,
trees standing alone, the shrubs in groups.
Air cools, light mellows, but summer heat
sticks to the stones of the retaining wall.
No evergreen is green forever.
No classes and no students until Fall,
then soon, ineluctably, none at all.

No vain regret for students who'll go
untaught, just mere facts of life and death.
Come September he'll see surprise
in his young colleagues' eyes.
One forgot himself last year
and blurted out, "You're still here?"

Here. What was here when he bought this house
decades ago? The magnolia, delicate
yet tough, hedges all around, a gnarled
juniper, three tall locusts of which just
one is left, that archaic thorny rose
by the fence, sole survivor, he was told,
of a thicket, the holly tree that died and,
yards away, a bush that also palled to
brittle brown, a phalanx of forsythia,
springtime's gold, the laurel, rhododendrons,
grass. But he had sown much more, planlessly,
seed by seed, with gifts, others' rejects, fresh
purchases that now had the *feng shui* of

familiarity. When the two locusts died,
he asked the garden store for quick
growing replacements and lugged home
a brace of arborvitae. He could recollect
digging the big holes, stripping the burlap
from their roots. Now he smiled before the
house-high hulks he had hefted easily
when they were young, when he was younger.
He calls the roll as he walks. Shrub roses,
jasmine, phlox, peonies, four spirea,
ground-covering myrtle, three flourishing
shrubs, *nomen ignotum.* But his favorites
are the Hosta, many and common,
easy-going perennials that nothing
eats, so fecund that, when their pale flowers
turn, he has to gather their seeds to forestall
their occupying every inch of lawn.
Yes, he likes the dozens of Hosta best.
But why?

A rabbi once asked a class of boys.
"Which is the most important holiday?"
Eager hands shot up like
reeds trembling in the wind.
"Yom Kippur!" "Passover!" "Rosh Hashanah!"
To each the old man shook his head.
"The Sabbath," is what the rabbi said.
"But, Rabbi, the Sabbath comes every week."
"And who is more important to you?
The aunts and uncles you see
see maybe once a year,
or the parents you see every day?"

Tending the garden, planting seeds,
Watering seedlings, yanking weeds,
checking for growth. It's like teaching.
Decades spent nurturing pupil and herb
always keeping in mind that
to teach is a transitive verb.

What will take root, which will wither
and turn a doltish, sickly brown?
Trees can fall—lightning took one down.
Which students will yawn, which fall asleep?
In office hours which might weep?

The holly was sawn down to the ground
yet the roots lived, a new plant grew;
and so, with the young. He often found
with cultivation, patience, help,
a dullard could turn things around
and, like the stump, become something new.

Classes need more cleverness than plants,
but both require empathy, patience,
a touch of fantasy, sharp secateurs.
Gardens are of the body, sweat, but
the reward is quick if straightness and smooth
green please you. Lectures want cleverness,
shocks, for instances, to flabbergast.
A drunk on the subway is never boring.
Still, in garden or classroom success depends
on others. Plants, like sophomores, must do
their proper work. No plagiarizing in the soil
or essays. Light must be turned to tissue.
Now he must be steeled for the worst.

Retirement, incapacity, or death,
whichever shows up first.

Some things may remain.
Father, teacher, writer,
a life like an all-nighter.
He'll leave behind this garden,
bachelors of arts, flawed
books, a flawless daughter.
As for his name, like Keats,
he stoically foresees it
will be writ on water.

Six Snapshots of Social Life

The conversation downstairs blurs, rises,
falls; politely meaningless exchanges
swiftly disperse. Up in the bathroom, a
woman weeps, checks the mirror, mends her face.

Two strangers in a bar found they both watched
the same TV series. They had different
favorite characters and one despised the
finale. So, they drank up and left.

It's noisy in the Food Court. He totes
his tray to the table where she sits with
her roommates, who will never forgive him.
She peeks up but won't dare to say his name.

After Ben's cousin's bar mitzvah, Rabbi
Wise closed in on him. "A Catholic girl?
You do know I can't perform the service."
Ben gave his best Yiddish shrug. "So who asked?"

The dogs are more pleased to see each other
than their owners, who sit singly on benches
watching their darlings run free, leap about,
just pausing to pee and smell out new friends.

Once we were sure it was true, that he was
gone at last, we rushed to the streets, the square,
singing, dancing, embracing. One pretty
girl tore off a young cop's hat, gave him a kiss.

Suburban Silence

Suburban silence, sing to me
of dark green lawns and fireflies,
hushed rustling in the white oak tree
guarding the swings, the faded cries
of squealing girls and impish boys
now fast asleep, making no noise.

Lawn mowers and leaf blowers cool
in garages next to SUVs.
The windows of the Greenwood School
are dark as the deeps of far-off seas.
Parents argue, watch TV, fret,
have sex, perhaps a cigarette.

In these precincts good counts for less
than nice, honesty than success.
Neighbors conceal their offenses;
resentments stay behind fences.
Nice houses, lawns—but all keep shtum
about where the cash comes from.

The city's rumbling soundtrack's pricked
by gunshots, laughter, shrieking sirens,
by late buses, hookups, conflicts,
the city of the poor, the addicts,
hugged by its gated environs'
indifferent arms of stone and bricks.

A few lie anxious, wide awake,
worrying about the state of things.
In fear and trembling they quake,
staring up at smooth white ceilings,
listening as their green suburb sings
in silence that's inane, opaque.

Tomorrow's Poem

The Muse, up before the sun, will
shake me awake. "Wake up, you lout;
the iron's hot. Brush, take your pill,
breakfast, pee. Get up!" she'll shout

and I'll obey, dismiss the doubt
that she's no more than a dawn dream,
mythic close to this cursed drought,
that she's enceinte with form, with theme,

and will serve up both as I
dash to my desk, uncap my pen
and luminously versify.
Sure, she'll come tomorrow—that's when.

Waking in Wakefield

A Parisian morning, brioche, café
au lait, sunlight good for artists' bleary
eyes, descent of Montmartre, comme-il-faut,
at ten stopped for tea in a crowded
room, lacquered walls, imperial aromas
faint as attar from old perfume bottles,
Shanghai boiled over with Asian life,
at forenoon the high sun in Omsk dazzled,
glinting off ice and the girls' apple cheeks,
at 11:30 in palm shadows the torrid
Congo just suited me, deep green on a green
darker than the soybean shoots sprouting in
Nebraska where I squeezed my fist
around a bolus of rich prairie dirt,
sipping sweet date wine I drizzled
through my fingers fine sand in a suburb
of Samarkand—sharp shadows, muezzin—
will I ever forget the, ah, sixteen-
year-old hetaera in Manila who rolled my
stiff neck, met the rising anguish of my knots
with hands smooth and promising as inner
thighs—I think soft female giggling must
be earth's bravest sound for I heard it
still as I sank into a deep Vera Cruz siesta,
in Tralee I chose a heather-colored
cable-stitch, in Bond Street a pair of wing-tips,
the Jerusalem papers lay smartly
folded beside my glass of sweet tea in
fragrant Oran, an apéritif drunk

in old Karlsruhe set me up for the
three-course Attic banquet in a bistro
strung with Bacchus' grapes, Apollo's laurel,
not far from the Delphic Oracle, then
afterwards I strolled the Piazza Navona
refreshed by the whispering fountains and
surrounded by sussurant Roman gossip,
smoking half a postprandial Havana,
one Soho pale ale too many and something
unpleasant bawled in a dive near the Loop
lent the night a dizzy piquancy of peril
though by twelve the Southern Cross lit
my lonesome way down the blank boulevards
and pungent alleys of Montevideo . . .
that must be how I found my way here and
fell asleep in this square room, this narrow bed.

War Games of 1955

The toys we liked the best were guns,
our favorite movies were about
the War—our fathers', not the ones
about which there was any doubt.

German grenadiers and Japanese
marines crumpled before our lines.
We took steady aim on our knees
beneath Saipan palms and Argonne pines.

We all had army surplus gear,
Sundays watched *Victory at Sea.*
On December 7 of each year
our teachers intoned solemnly.

We joined the Cub Scouts just to wear
the uniform. But here's the truth:
zealotry made us unaware
we could have passed for Hitler Youth.

Ten years on, a different story,
fetid jungles, mines that maimed.
A few joined up, keen for glory.
The deferred? Grateful and ashamed.

When Is A Poem Not?

In a desiccated country some are counting
up the daily dead while others spruce
up their arguments that prove even
three-year-old bystanders aren't innocent.

Mrs. Oleander fears she's aging badly—
that is to say, she looks forty-five at
fifty and yet hasn't turned one whit wiser.
The spanking new Lexus cannot compensate.

At the playground, on the beach,
in the alley, by the pool, on the
field, by the river, children are
making their timeless children noises.

The teeming insect world appears indifferent
to everything but weather, hunger, sex, and light.
The beech trees obstinately decline to relocate.
Sad, how nature tries so hard to ignore history.

I am nothing, she whined, *nothing*.
Not so, I protested. You're really *something*.
She glared at me scornfully, pleased to deny
the thing she yearned most to believe.

Mr. Prixendieu once made good money,
used to feel as secure as a locked box
in a Greek Revival bank, with a portico.
Well, at least the bank's still there.

An intractable, insoluble, unreckonable
problem metastasized until it overflowed Joe's
mind, dribbled out of his mouth, spilled from
his ears, then careened down Route 95.

They had an ennui epidemic, a plague of melancholy,
a contagion of pyrexia, endemic pessimism,
febricity, calenture, megrims, tedium vitae—
until a huge sinkhole swallowed the whole town.

After the fourteenth PowerPoint presentation
our loyal employees rushed to the bar to drink
and compete to see who could be the most cynical.
The contest wound up in a dead drunk heat.

Give us wheat and hope, beef and grace,
potatoes and dignity, prayed the fervent priest
in a deep voice even louder and more
resonant than our rumbling tummies.

It'll be a *terrible* drive, Wanda warned. Yes, but so
so lovely when we get there, Chet cheerfully
replied. When we *get* there, she scoffed. *Idiot*,
we won't make it over the first bridge.

Would this be an essay if I insisted
ardently enough, albeit not a fine one?
Surely, it's neither a poem nor a prayer.
And, after all, *essay* merely means *attempt*.
Yellow Moon at Lake WeishanYellow Moon at Lake Weishan

On the Road Near Chiangling the Poet Chen Hsi-wei Encounters a Young Musician, Summer 597 A.D.

Tallow leaves hang low, grass is brittle underfoot.
Birds spiral lazily then flutter down in the shade.
Prickly lettuce and withered jasmine
lie flat, like bing cakes baking on the dirt.
Paving tiles burn right through straw sandals.

Her eyes are so alert, it's as if she just found them.
The heat barely touches her, this devotee of song.
She's not the sort to compromise, not yet.
She asks me about music, what I've heard and whom.
Did I hear the great Zhang Chu in the capital?

Her reverence for her art exalts them both. She's
sure a celestial melody floats just above her head;
if only she could tug it down and play it then
the world would certainly change for the good.
The sun wouldn't scorch, perhaps taxes would drop.

She is small, delicate, nearly a child, though
if you look closely, you'll see that's half true,
that she's a soft soul in a hard cocoon.
Her faith is as unspoiled as her smooth skin.
Who would dare to scoff? Not me.

She asks my name and when I give it
I'm startled. She bows low, calls me Master,

can hardly believe it, tells me how much she
loves my old poem about Lake Weishan.
Her face is fervent as a praying monk's.

Taking up her liuqin, she begins to sing
and it's like running water by a dusty road.
I feel my forgotten poem surfacing from
Lake Weishan itself transformed, summoned
by the sudden beauty of this butterfly.

Yellow Moon at Lake Weishan

Weishan lies cool and still as a forgotten bowl of tea,
the moon immobile as a yellow disk embroidered
on a gown of black silk heavy with pearls.
As time is change, so these motionless bamboo leaves,
these reeds standing to attention like proud veterans,
yield a moment without war, decay, turmoil or age.

I too am still in this moment, captivated by
the moonlight on the enchanted lake, silver and gold.
The moon's light on the water looks so precious and lovable,
I reach out to touch it and so, with my foolish hand,
spoil eternal peace.
Alas! If only I had refrained.

Hsi-wei Records Ten-Year Old Mai Ling's Good Idea

Long ago, between Night and Day there was war.
They taunted and insulted one another. Spite and spleen.
Like a woolen curtain, Night sought to black out Day
while Day, like a huge bonfire, labored to outshine moon and stars.
From these mighty battles, people and animals suffered,
enjoying a little respite only at noon and midnight.

With Winter and Summer it was much the same.
They detested each other and all the more
for being evenly matched. Midsummer and Midwinter
were calm, but, in between, the seasons' wrestled ceaselessly;
tempests and earthquakes afflicted the world.

One day, as her parents were complaining,
Mai Ling, a little girl of ten years, spoke up.
"Nobody can tell me what time is or how much there is of it.
Why not just make more? Then Uncle Winter can have
his time and Auntie Summer hers; then Day can be day
all day and Night can be night the whole night through."

Mai Ling's parents laughed indulgently, as parents will.
But her old granny reproached them. "Listen to the child.
New eyes see better than old ones." And so
the people convened a parley with Day and Night,
with Winter and Summer, and let Mai Ling explain.

"Uncle Day, when you get sleepy you shouldn't struggle.
Auntie Night, when you're worn out, you ought to go to bed.
You shouldn't rub your eyes and spite each other.
Neighbors need boundaries, little walls, not too high.
We can make new time if only you'll agree.
We'll set fences between you: Dusk and Dawn.

"And as for you, Uncle Winter and Auntie Summer,
you should do the same and not rub up against each other
ruining our rice with mistimed warmth and blasts of cold,
hail and sleet, too much rain or parching heat.
Let's set new seasons between you, just little ones, low walls.
As Winter tires, we'll have Spring, and as Summer fades, Fall.
That is my idea. In the night people and animals shall
sleep and during the day we'll work and play.
In Spring we'll sow and in the Fall harvest.
Then you can stop this nasty wrangling and enjoy yourselves.
Then we shall all be grateful to you, blessing
each day and each night, every season and every year."

Hsi-wei in the Gardens of Shun

I passed through Shun last year in the
month of blossoms when new leaves made
the katsura branches look like mist.
The Duke's chamberlain summoned me.
We took tea then meandered through
the palace's renowned gardens.
Lord Zhang Tsu, my host, spoke of
the Orchid Pavillion Gathering. He asked if
I had ever seen the calligraphy of Wang Xizhi.

Behind the peonies stood a small pagoda,
an elegant thing, feminine and blue.
There the noblewomen of Shun stood together
swaying silkenly, like willows, shy as foals.
I found it hard not to look at them.
With a smile, the Chamberlain remarked
that, as Shun's ladies spoke only in demure
whispers, one would have to draw quite
near to hear their slanderous gossip.

Hsi-wei's Justice

Lord Zhang Siyu paced grumpily until
his second wife set things right with
no more than a small adjustment to his sash.

Meiling waited until her brother got up
to pee then moved her toy duck
to the right side of her yellow pillow.

Wu's mother-in-law looked at what her son's
new wife had done: nothing in its proper place.
Uncomplaining, she put all the pots to rights.

The world's a wavering rope-walker whose
apparent stability is really the ceaseless
setting right of countless imbalances.

The Mogwai

The spirits of the unjustly slain appear when
slowly falling flakes quiet the world,
on afternoons so sultry even the diligent leave work,
above the peonies in gardens, beneath the plum blossoms,
between courses when the guests are full of yellow wine.
But mostly it is at night that they stand by beds
hissing their rebukes, accusations, denunciations,
lurking in corners doorways, colonnades.

No one sees them skulking about save
those who cannot stop seeing them.

People say they can be mollified by burning money,
placated with prayers, assuaged by sacrifices.
They say these things the way mothers console children
as flood waters rise, the earth quakes and tiles fall,
when droughts bring famine that swell their bellies,
when ruthless bandits bellow through their villages;
but, like these, the mogwai are not to be appeased.
They are implacable as the law, thirsty for revenge.
Nothing will appease them but confession and punishment.

No one hears their condemnations save
those who cannot stop hearing them.

The War in the South

Were you ready for them? People say you weren't warned.
What a shock it must have been after the easy triumphs,
the delicious exotic food I picture you wolfing down
as you lounged in the abandoned palaces of Tong Binh.
Was the food as good as they say? Are the women of
Linyi really slim as willow branches, shy as fawns?

Champa must have beckoned like a crimson pomegranate
hanging so low you only needed to raise your hand, tug,
and drop it in the basket of the Emperor's swelling glory.

But how terrifying they must have been, the war elephants,
their tusks and exultation, the thick trunks rearing back
like giant pythons seeking prey, the cracking of their
rush through the forest. The biggest trees would
be nothing to them, mere twigs and splinters.

Many must have been crushed, broken, shouldered aside.
But you officers, steady men and crafty, didn't panic, not you.
You passed the order to feign retreat, found soft earth and
arrayed the ranks of crossbowmen, set the men to digging.
Elephants are no fools. I imagine only the first stumbled into
the traps; the others wheeled slowly and fled, harried by bolts,
stamping on the infantry of Champa. What a paean the
men must have raised, seeing war's fortune turn.

They say many victories drew you deeper into the poisonous
southern forests. First a few fell ill, crying pitiably for
water. Then more and yet more until the whole army was

wasted by fevers. The news has come home but few of you.
Old men and boys, mothers and young girls, weep as they plant
this year's rice and till brown fields, missing your strength.

They say that in Daxing the Emperor has met with his ministers.

I know we parted six years ago. Only in dreams do
we still drink under the new moon, joking, reciting verses;
yet to me also the world feels like a forsaken field.

Yuan Boling, you triumphed over the enormous but fell to
the invisible. Surely there must be some lesson in that.

Autumn in the Yellow Mountains

Deep in a golden grove on the riverbank
a slender lady in a silken gown sits with her maid.
Both look out at a drifting sampan; the
inattentive boatman has dropped his oar.
The lady holds her hand to her mouth.
If I were that boatman I too would fail
to see the laughing lady and her maid
among the vivid leaves and twisting boughs.
My gaze too would be fixed higher, on the
waterfall like molten silver, the crooked
Huangshan pines, the rocks upholding all.
Leaves turn and fall. We laugh and drift
and soon are gone. Mountains endure.

The Silence of Hermits

One winter morning I watched two hermits sitting together.
Luo Nianzu had come to pay a visit to Bao Sying.
I prepared tea. For a serene hour they faced each other
on the cold dirt floor, sipping tea, saying not one word.
I recall it as a beautiful hour, lovely, full and
still as Lake Weishan when the dawn mist lifts.

I learned how much can be said by saying nothing.
Silence may be noisy with gossip, jokes, endearments
when the silent are in perfect accord. That's how it is
with lovers, likewise those whose lives have brought them
to the same wisdom—lovers linked by feeling, sages by thought.
Such silences surpass even the verses of Qu Yuan.

The Little Straw Sandals

Mrs. Chu ordered sandals for her grandson
Wanglei. She beamed, proud that the boy could
Already walk. "They'll be his first," she said.
She took something from the pocket of her skirt.
It was a little Wanglei-sole-sized cucumber.
"This is how small you're to make them."

Fashioning such tiny sandals isn't simple.
I used the finest straw, pulled the strands
Taut, made the knots tight, and carefully sliced
off the loose ends. I made them sturdy too.
Wanglei was bound to be rough on them.
Straw sandals are humble, useful, honest ,
Like Mrs. Chu who tried to pay me.

I've had more customers than readers.
I like when people admire their new sandals,
Hold them up, turn them this way and that,
And say it must have been hard to make them.
But I'm even happier when they say that
Making straw sandals must be easy for me.
To tell the truth, it's no different with my poems.

Yuan-yang

A pair of ducks flapping wings in unison
fly over the muddy field. Zhang digs
furrows and Mei follows, dropping seeds.
Zhang raises his eyes, shades them with his hand.
"Yuan-yang!" he cries. Mei looks up and, for
a moment, it's their wedding day again.

Long ago, the ducks signified brotherly love.
It's not true that symbols can never change.
The Shijing masters shifted the love of
brothers to that between a constant man
and his faithful wife. Yet symbols also
cannot change. Brother or spouse, Yuang-yang
signifies loyalty, fidelity, an
intimacy exclusive as the Emperor's
bedchamber in the Palace of Renshou.

These ducks, people fondly say, mate for life.
His raiment is an extravagant rainbow
of orange, purple, green, and black feathers.
His beak is delicate, his eyes jet-black.
She is as big as he, but demurely dressed
in ash-gray with white speckles on her
modest breast. They are so well-matched, to see
them swimming side-by-side is a delight.
To catch the rare sight of the pair in flight
is warranted to bring good luck.

An old peasant in Liangzhou, one who had
long watched Yuang-yang come and go, told me the
truth. "Just one summer," he whispered for fear
his wife might hear. "New mates every Fall."

Symbols soar above our muddy, bloody fields.
Though our feet are fixed firmly in the dirt,
it's not wrong, from time to time, to look up.

Hsi-wei's Last Poem

Yesterday I had a visitor, a young lord declaring he wants
to become a poet. His well-fed body was bent with humility,
yet his eyes glittered with intelligence and ambition.
"Come sit," I said to calm him but he stood and recited
one poem, then another. "Not bad at all," I said appreciatively,
not wishing to discourage the lad. Embarrassed, he bowed
and in a voice like that of a mother's putting her child to bed,
said, "But Master, they are yours." Then I made tea and we
sat watching the moon rise, talking of the Shijing masters.

How strange now to think of all those li I walked,
the provinces I traversed. By now, all my straw sandals
will have turned to dust, worn out by the feet of hard-working
peasants. Strange too to think of the poems I wrote long ago
and can no longer remember. They too will become so
much wind-borne chaff, having also served their uses.
Poems and sandals are all I made, workman-like things,
so many footsteps on dry roads, waiting for the rain.

From my little courtyard I used to watch the sun and moon,
then it was the days I observed; now it is whole seasons
marching in review. Like rainwater as it nears a drain,
time has begun to race, each year a smaller fraction of
my life. The mountain turns from green to brown to
white so swiftly that I believe a pair of old monks
beginning their ascent in springtime would be lost in
snowbanks long before they glimpsed the top.

www.ingramcontent.com/pod-product-compliance
Ingram Content Group UK Ltd.
Pitfield, Milton Keynes, MK11 3LW, UK
UKHW041315190726
13845UKWH00025B/289